# ◫ READERS

## Level 3

## Level 4

# A Note to Parents

DK READERS is a compelling program for beginning readers, designed in conjunction with leading literacy experts, including Dr. Linda Gambrell, Distinguished Professor of Education at Clemson University. Dr. Gambrell has served as President of the National Reading Conference, the College Reading Association, and the International Reading Association.

Beautiful illustrations and superb full-color photographs combine with engaging, easy-to-read stories to offer a fresh approach to each subject in the series. Each DK READER is guaranteed to capture a child's interest while developing his or her reading skills, general knowledge, and love of reading.

The five levels of DK READERS are aimed at different reading abilities, enabling you to choose the books that are exactly right for your child:

**Pre-level 1:** Learning to read
**Level 1:** Beginning to read
**Level 2:** Beginning to read alone
**Level 3:** Reading alone
**Level 4:** Proficient readers

The "normal" age at which a child begins to read can be anywhere from three to eight years old. Adult participation through the lower levels is very helpful for providing encouragement, discussing storylines, and sounding out unfamiliar words.

No matter which level you select, you can be sure that you are helping your child learn to read, then read to learn!

LONDON, NEW YORK, MUNICH,
MELBOURNE, and DELHI

**Editorial Assistant** Ruth Amos
**Senior Editor** Elizabeth Dowsett
**Designers** Jon Hall, Sandra Perry
**Pre-Production Producer** Marc Staples
**Producer** Louise Daly
**Publishing Manager** Julie Ferris
**Design Manager** Nathan Martin
**Art Director** Ron Stobbart
**Publishing Director** Simon Beecroft

**Reading Consultant**
Linda B. Gambrell, Ph.D.

Dorling Kindersley would like to thank:
Randi Sørensen at the LEGO Group and J. W. Rinzler,
Leland Chee, Troy Alders, and Carol Roeder at Lucasfilm.

First published in the United States in 2013
by DK Publishing
375 Hudson Street, New York, New York 10014

10 9 8 7 6 5 4 3 2 1
001–181490–July/13

Page design copyright © 2013 Dorling Kindersley Limited

DK books are available at special discounts when purchased
in bulk for sales promotions, premiums, fund-raising,
or educational use.
For details, contact:
DK Publishing Special Markets,
375 Hudson Street, New York, New York 10014
SpecialSales@dk.com

A catalog record for this book is available
from the Library of Congress.

ISBN: 978-1-4654-0869-3 (Paperback)
ISBN: 978-1-4654-0870-9 (Hardcover)

Color reproduction by Altaimage, UK
Printed and bound in China by L.Rex

Discover more at
**www.dk.com**
**www.starwars.com**
**www.LEGO.com/starwars**

# Contents

# DK READERS

READING
3
ALONE

**LEGO STAR WARS**

# REVENGE OF THE SITH ™

Written by Elizabeth Dowsett

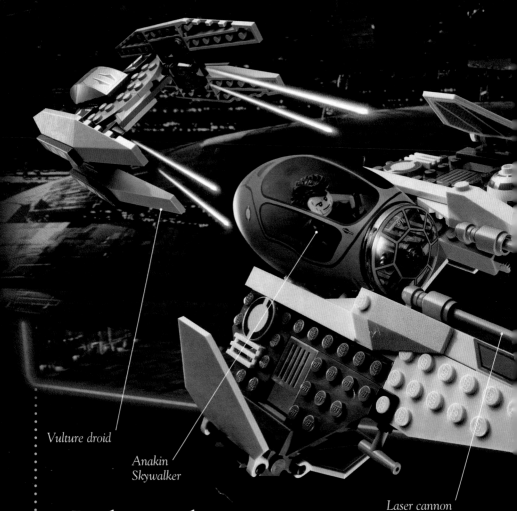

Vulture droid

Anakin
Skywalker

Laser cannon

# Jedi to the rescue!

The leader of the galaxy has been
kidnapped! His name is Palpatine and
he is the Supreme Chancellor of the
Republic.

Rescuing the Chancellor is a job for
the Jedi! Jedi keep peace in the galaxy.

Here comes a Jedi Knight now!
This is Anakin Skywalker in his
yellow Jedi Interceptor. He is zooming
to rescue Chancellor Palpatine,
but he'd better watch
out—there is a vicious
vulture droid on his tail!
Don't worry—Anakin is a very
skilled pilot and he can easily
outwit a vulture droid. He dodges its
fire and blasts it using the laser
cannons on his Interceptor. Boom!

**Jedi Knight**
Anakin has the talent
to become a great Jedi,
but he is often impulsive.
Jedi must control their
feelings and they must
try not to become angry
or greedy.

# Buzz droid attack

Another Jedi is on his way to rescue Chancellor Palpatine. This is Obi-Wan Kenobi in his red Jedi Interceptor. Obi-Wan is Anakin's brave Jedi Master.

Watch out! A trifighter droid has released a swarm of buzz droids.

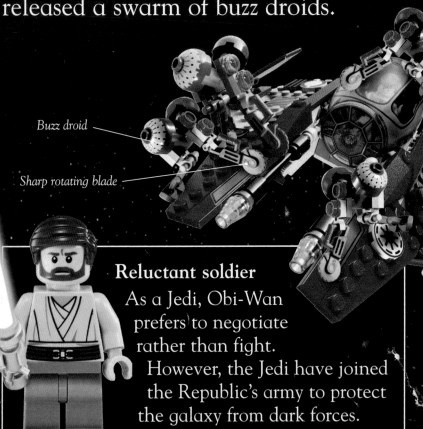

Buzz droid

Sharp rotating blade

### Reluctant soldier

As a Jedi, Obi-Wan prefers to negotiate rather than fight.

However, the Jedi have joined the Republic's army to protect the galaxy from dark forces.

Buzz droids may be small, but they are deadly. They swarm over Obi-Wan's spaceship and attack it with their spinning blades. No matter how much Obi-Wan rocks his ship, he cannot shake them off!

Anakin bumps Obi-Wan's ship, and the buzz droids go flying! Anakin has saved his Master!

Trifighter droid

Chancellor Palpatine

# Deadly duel

Obi-Wan and Anakin have found Chancellor Palpatine on a giant Separatist starship, but their work is not over yet. Palpatine is guarded by Count Dooku. Count Dooku used to be a Jedi, but now he is the evil leader of the Separatists.

Obi-Wan duels Dooku with his lightsaber, but is soon injured.

Anakin fights on alone and overpowers Dooku. The Jedi always show mercy to their enemies, but Palpatine tells Anakin to destroy Dooku. Anakin is not sure, but then follows Palpatine's orders. Now Count Dooku is no more!

*Count Dooku*

**Evil allies**

The Separatists are a group of greedy people who want to rule the galaxy.

The Separatists are secretly controlled by Dooku's mysterious cloaked master. He is called Darth Sidious.

*Hologram of Darth Sidious*

# Beware the dark side!

The Force is an energy that runs through all living things. The Jedi study the Force, and it gives them special powers. The Jedi use these skills to ensure peace and justice in the galaxy.

Mace Windu

Obi-Wan Kenobi

Anakin Skywalker

Yoda

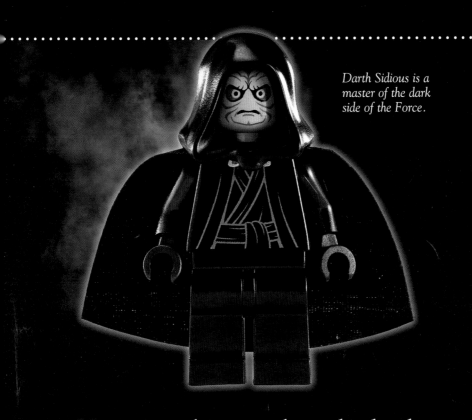

*Darth Sidious is a master of the dark side of the Force.*

However, there is also a bad side to the Force, fueled by anger and hate. The Sith are greedy warriors who use the dark side. It gives them deadly powers to attack their enemies, but at a terrible cost.

If you give in to the temptations of the dark side, its power will take over you. Your body and mind will become twisted with evil.

# A dangerous path

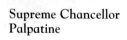

Everyone knows Palpatine as the wise Chancellor of the Republic, but he is hiding a terrible secret. He is actually the Sith Lord called Darth Sidious and he is plotting to seize control of the galaxy.

Supreme Chancellor Palpatine

Palpatine wants Anakin to be his Sith apprentice. He tempts the young Jedi down the path to the dark side by tricking him.

The leader of the Jedi, Yoda, tries to warn Anakin, but he will not listen. Anakin is too full of rage. He is angry with the Jedi because they don't give him the power he craves.

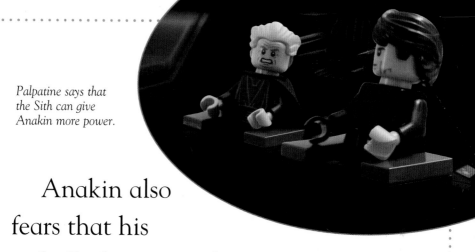

*Palpatine says that the Sith can give Anakin more power.*

Anakin also fears that his wife, Padmé, is in danger. Palpatine tells Anakin that the dark side can keep her safe.

Will Anakin listen to Palpatine's lies? Will he give in to the temptations of the dark side?

*Yoda tries to warn Anakin about the dark side.*

# Double agent?

The twelve wisest Jedi Masters form the Jedi Council and they guide the Jedi Order in keeping the peace.

Chancellor Palpatine appoints Anakin to the Council so that he can spy on the Jedi for him.

Anakin Skywalker

Kit Fisto

Obi-Wan Kenobi

Yoda

The Jedi Council is led by Grand Master Yoda.

The Jedi let Anakin join the
Council, because they want Anakin
to spy on Palpatine for them!
They have become very suspicious of
the Chancellor.

Anakin is caught in the middle!
What will he do? Which side will he
choose now?

Saesee Tiin

Mace Windu

*Yellow markings for Star Corps trooper*

**Speeder bike**

# The clone army

Dark times have fallen. The Republic is fighting the Separatists. The Grand Army of the Republic is made up of Jedi generals and millions

*Red marking for clone shock trooper*

of clone troopers.

Clone troopers are identical human clones who are specially bred and trained to fight for the Republic without question.

**Breeding ground**
Clone troopers are
grown and trained
together in a special
base on the planet
of Kamino.

Clone troopers wear white armor
with color markings depending on
their unit.

They go into battle on vehicles
such as speeder bikes and
strong, armored walkers.

The clones fight
the Separatist droid
army with deadly
blaster weapons.

Blaster

*The AT-RT is an All Terrain Recon
Transport two-legged walker.*

# What is a Wookiee?

Who are these hairy creatures? These are two Wookiees named Chewbacca and Tarfful. Wookiees may look scary, but they are brave and loyal to the Republic.

Wookiees have always lived on the peaceful planet of Kashyyyk, but it is not peaceful anymore! The Separatists are attacking the Wookiees' homeland with their fearsome metal army.

Chewbacca

Tarfful

Thousands of battle droids and super battle droids invade Kashyyyk with deadly spider droids and huge, threatening tank droids. A big battle is brewing.

Battle droid

STAP vehicle

Super battle droid

Transport carrier

Tank droid

Spider droid

# The Battle of Kashyyyk

Hurrah! Jedi Master Yoda has arrived on Kashyyyk with the clone army to help the Wookiees defend their planet.

The Separatists launch a fierce attack with their tank droids. The clone troopers fight back valiantly on swamp speeders and walkers. They ride on top of their tall two-legged walkers and fire powerful blaster cannons.

The Wookiees are battling for their planet, with their unique vehicles and weapons.

*Fluttercraft*

*Separatist tank droid*

The Wookiees hover over the battlefield in their patrol planes called fluttercraft, and they fire at the battle droids with bowcasters.

**Wookiee weapons**
Wookiees use the plentiful wood on their forest planet to create unique weapons like this bowcaster.

# General Grievous

What a strange sight! This four-armed creature is a vicious cyborg named General Grievous. He is ruthless and very, very fierce. Grievous is the Commander of the droid army and he takes his orders from Darth Sidious.

Obi-Wan has come to the planet Utapau to hunt Grievous down, but it will not be an easy mission.

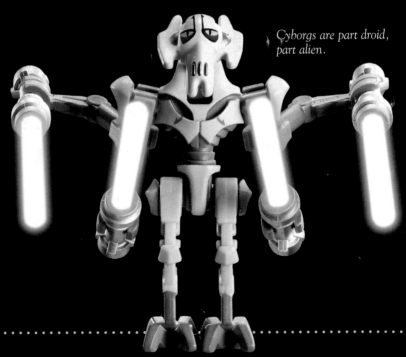

*Cyborgs are part droid, part alien.*

Grievous is not a Jedi, but he is very skilled at using a lightsaber. He wields not one, but four! He whirls them in four different directions at once. Obi-Wan must use all his courage and training to fight him.

*Darth Sidious gives Grievous secret battle orders via hologram.*

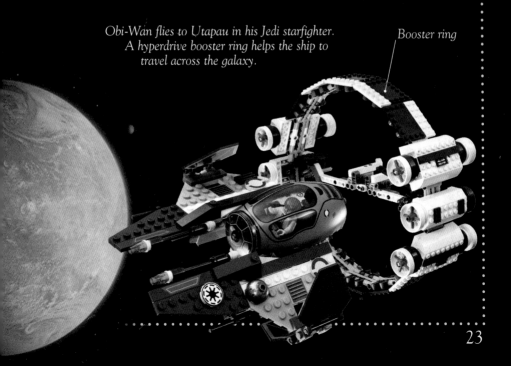

*Obi-Wan flies to Utapau in his Jedi starfighter. A hyperdrive booster ring helps the ship to travel across the galaxy.*

*Booster ring*

# Deadly chase

Cowardly General Grievous leaps onto a huge wheel bike and whooshes away from Obi-Wan. Grievous's wheel bike can run on four robotic legs, or fold up and roll on its big wheel. Obi-Wan will not let Grievous escape, but how can he keep up?

Obi-Wan jumps onto a varactyl's back and rides off in hot pursuit. Varactyls are large reptiles with a spiky head and a long tail.

Grievous puts up a vicious fight, but Obi-Wan keeps on following him. After a dangerous duel, Obi-Wan defeats Grievous. Victory to the Jedi!

# Palpatine's arrest

Chancellor Palpatine's cover is blown! The Jedi have realized that their leader is really a Sith Lord. He has been manipulating the Republic so that he can take over the galaxy.

Powerful Jedi Master Mace Windu leads a strike force to Palpatine's office to challenge him.

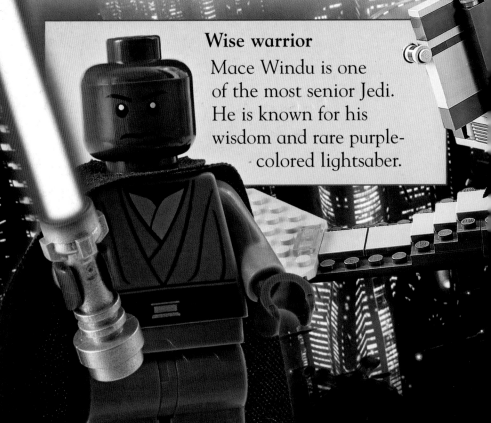

**Wise warrior**
Mace Windu is one of the most senior Jedi. He is known for his wisdom and rare purple-colored lightsaber.

The Jedi believe in justice, so they
plan to arrest the Chancellor and put
him on trial. But Palpatine attacks!
He strikes the Jedi with his
red-bladed lightsaber until just Mace
is left standing.

Mace is powerful, but is
Palpatine more powerful?

*Jedi Saesee Tiin*

*Jedi Kit Fisto*    *Jedi Agen Kolar*

**Chancellor
Palpatine's office**

# Lightning strike

Here comes Anakin! He can save
Mace and destroy Palpatine once and
for all. But, wait! Anakin is not sure...
He doesn't know which side to take.

Scars

Palpatine
summons the dark
power of the Force
and zaps crackling
bolts of blue
lightning from his
fingertips. Mace is
quick and deflects the
lightning with his lightsaber,
bouncing it back at Palpatine.
The powerful blue bolts scar his face.

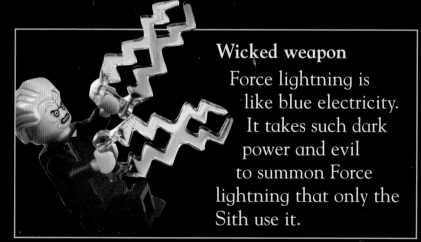

**Wicked weapon**
Force lightning is
like blue electricity.
It takes such dark
power and evil
to summon Force
lightning that only the
Sith use it.

# Anakin's choice

Anakin chooses to side with Palpatine, but he doesn't really want to hurt Mace.

However, Anakin believes that the dark side of the Force is the only way to keep Padmé safe from danger.

Anakin takes up his lightsaber
against his fellow Jedi, Mace.
Wicked Palpatine grabs his chance
and blasts Mace out of the window
with deadly Force lightning.
Anakin has betrayed the Jedi.
His journey to the dark
side is now complete.

**Arise, Darth Vader!**
Anakin is now Darth
Sidious's apprentice
and is renamed
Darth Vader.
Anakin Skywalker
is no more!

# Order 66

The clone army is trained to be completely obedient. Clone troopers must follow any order from the Chancellor of the Republic without question. That person is Palpatine and he has betrayed the Jedi.

Palpatine is pretending that the Jedi want to overthrow the Republic. He issues Order 66: The clones are commanded to destroy the Jedi!

*Lucky Obi-Wan escapes from the clones who attack him on Utapau, but other Jedi are not so lucky.*

Across the galaxy, clone troopers turn on their Jedi leaders. The Jedi need to watch out!

Yoda is too powerful for the clones on Kashyyyk. He gives them a taste of their own medicine!

# A new Galactic Empire

Palpatine has seized control of the whole galaxy and destroyed the Republic! In its place, he creates a new Empire, with himself as Emperor. He is the sole leader and no one can challenge him now!

As Palpatine's apprentice, Darth Vader will be his second-in-command in the new Empire.

Emperor Palpatine
declares his new Empire to the
Senate. He announces that the Jedi
are now the galaxy's enemy number
one. No Jedi is safe!

*Obi-Wan and Yoda are heartbroken to
discover the terrible things that Anakin has
done, and that he has joined the Emperor.*

# Yoda versus Darth Sidious

Who will stop the Emperor and his wicked plans? Yoda is very powerful, despite his small size. If anyone can stop Darth Sidious, Yoda can!

*Yoda and Darth Sidious battle one-on-one.*

Yoda confronts Sidious in the
Senate building on Coruscant.
They battle each other with
crackling lightsabers in a mighty
duel. Sidious strikes Yoda with
powerful Sith lightning, but Yoda
bounces it back at the Sith Lord.

The light side of the Force gives
Yoda special powers, but even
he cannot defeat Darth Sidious's
evil. Neither warrior can win.
Yoda must retreat.

**Master of the Force**
Yoda's small body is
over 900 years old,
but he is so strong
in the Force that he
wields great power.

*Darth Sidious no longer needs the
Separatists. He sends Darth Vader to the
planet Mustafar in his green Jedi Interceptor
to destroy the Separatist leaders hiding there.*

# Mission to Mustafar

Mustafar is a hot, fiery
planet with rivers of boiling
lava. Here Obi-Wan tries
to stop Darth Vader. It is
not too late for him to
return to the light side of
the Force, but Vader will not
listen to him. Left with no
choice, Obi-Wan must fight
his friend.

The pair have a dangerous
lightsaber battle over bubbling pools
of boiling hot lava.

*Vader balances on a mining
droid used to collect rocks
on Mustafar.*

# Triumph and loss

On Mustafar, Obi-Wan gains the upper hand in the duel with Darth Vader and wounds his former student.

Obi-Wan triumphs over Darth Vader and wins the battle, but he is not happy.

*Vader's body is so injured, he surely cannot survive.*

Obi-Wan is heartbroken by Vader's betrayal of the Jedi and his fall to the dark side. Obi-Wan feels like he has lost a brother. However, there is nothing he can do to help Vader. He flies away from Mustafar, leaving Vader's badly burned body behind.

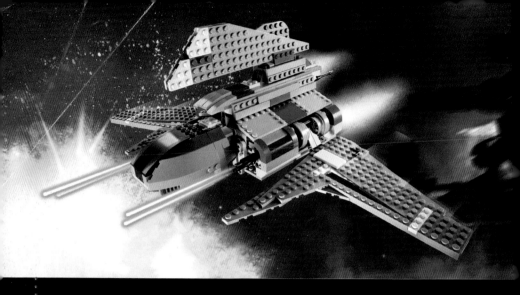

# Sith rescue

Darth Sidious senses through the Force that his apprentice, Darth Vader, is in trouble. He rushes to the planet Mustafar in his Imperial shuttle and finds Vader lying by the lava. He is gravely injured.

**Imperial bodyguards**
The Emperor is escorted by clone troopers in V-wing fighters as a mark of his importance.

Sidious orders a
clone trooper to
carry Vader onto
the Imperial shuttle.
The shuttle flies back to
Coruscant, escorted by
clone troopers in V-wing fighters.
Onboard the shuttle, a 2-1B
medical droid attends to Vader's
badly damaged and burned body.

*2-1B medical droid*

# Darth Vader reborn

Darth Vader is so badly injured from his duel with Obi-Wan that his body cannot live without the help of machinery. The medical droids create a special suit of black armor to protect Vader's body and a mask to help him breathe.

*FX medical droid*

Who is this person? Once upon a time, he was Anakin Skywalker, but that person is no longer recognizable. He is full of rage and fear because he has lost Padmé—the dark side could not keep her safe after all. He has a new body and a new name.

Darth Vader's journey to the dark side of the Force is complete.

# The Death Star

The Emperor has taken over the galaxy with his new Sith apprentice. Yoda and Obi-Wan are in hiding, and the Jedi Order is destroyed. Darth Sidious's plan is almost complete! Now he just needs to finish building a new gigantic super weapon called the Death Star.

The Death Star is a battle station the size of a small moon and it is armed with a deadly laser beam. Its superlaser has enough power to destroy an entire planet in one hit.

Darth Vader and his master stand side by side, watching as their fearsome new weapon is created. Soon it will be ready...

### A new hope?

Can anyone stand up to the Emperor? Padmé did not survive, but she had two twins named Luke and Leia. For now they are safely hidden, but maybe one day Luke and Leia can defeat the Sith. The future of the galaxy depends on them!

Leia and Luke

# Glossary

**Appoints**
Assigns or nominates to a position or job.

**Apprentice**
Student or pupil.

**Betrayed**
Broke another person's trust or behaved in a disloyal way.

**Clones**
Identical copies of one person or thing.

**Confronts**
Questions or challenges.

**Craves**
Desires or wishes for.

**Declares**
Announces or proclaims.

**Deflects**
Turns away, bounces back, or diverts.

**Droids**
Metal robots.

**Empire**
A group of nations ruled over by one leader, who is called an Emperor.

**Escorted**
Guarded or traveled with someone to protect them.

**Galaxy**
A group of millions of stars and planets.

**Hologram**
A 3-D image of a person who is not physically there. It is used as a way to communicate.

**Impulsive**
When a person reacts or takes action quickly without thinking first.

**Kidnapped**
Captured and taken away as a prisoner.

**Manipulating**
Controlling or changing something in a secretive way.

**Negotiate**
To work or talk with others in order to solve a problem together.

**Outwit**
To get the better of somebody or to outsmart them.

**Overthrow**
To defeat or topple.

**Plotting**
Secretly creating a plan, often a bad or evil one.

**Republic**
A nation or group of nations in which the people vote for their leaders.

**Retreat**
Leave or flee from a duel or battle.

**Ruthless**
Without mercy.

**Senate**
A group of people who govern the Republic together.

**STAP**
Single Trooper Aerial Platform. A vehicle used by droids for transport.

**Strike force**
A team of soldiers or warriors who are sent out on a specific mission.

**Summons**
Gathers or musters.

**Suspicious**
Doubtful, wary, or not trusting in something or somebody.

**Temptations**
Attractive things that are desirable or enticing.

**Triumph**
Victory or success.

**Unique**
Special, one-of-a-kind, or unusual.

**Unit**
A group or regiment within an army.

**Vicious**
Spiteful or wicked.

**Wields**
Holds or brandishes an item, often a weapon.

# Index